D1524420

Komodo Dragons

Leo Statts

abdopublishing.com

Published by Abdo Zoom™, PO Box 398166, Minneapolis, Minnesota 55439. Copyright © 2017 by Abdo Consulting Group, Inc. International copyrights reserved in all countries. No part of this book may be reproduced in any form without written permission from the publisher. Abdo Zoom™ is a trademark and logo of Abdo Consulting Group, Inc.

Printed in the United States of America, North Mankato, Minnesota
062016
092016

Cover Photo: Richard Susanto/Shutterstock Images
Interior Photos: Eric Isselee/Shutterstock Images, 1; Shutterstock Images, 4, 9; David Evison/Shutterstock Images, 5; Sergey Uryadnikov/Shutterstock Images, 7; Moroz Nataliya/Shutterstock Images, 8; Rafal Cichawa/iStockphoto, 10–11; Red Line Editorial, 11, 20 (left), 20 (right), 21 (left), 21 (right); Gudkov Andrey/Shutterstock Images, 12; Pius Lee/Shutterstock Images, 13; Edmund Lowe Photography/Shutterstock Images, 15; Mike Lane/iStockphoto, 16; Karen Pulfer Focht/The Commercial Appeal/AP Images, 17; Kjersti Joergensen/Shutterstock Images, 18

Editor: Brienna Rossiter
Series Designer: Madeline Berger
Art Direction: Dorothy Toth

Publisher's Cataloging-in-Publication Data
Names: Statts, Leo, author.
Title: Komodo dragons / by Leo Statts.
Description: Minneapolis, MN : Abdo Zoom, [2017] | Series: Desert animals |
    Includes bibliographical references and index.
Identifiers: LCCN 2016941141 | ISBN 9781680791822 (lib. bdg.) |
    ISBN 9781680793505 (ebook) | ISBN 9781680794397 (Read-to-me ebook)
Subjects: LCSH: Komodo dragons--Juvenile literature.
Classification: DDC 597.95--dc23
LC record available at http://lccn.loc.gov/2016941141

Table of Contents

Komodo Dragons

Komodo dragons are reptiles.
They are cold-blooded.

Their mouths are filled with bacteria.

They bite their prey.
Bacteria goes into
the bite. This helps
kill the prey.

Komodo dragons have short legs. They have thick bodies.

Their tails are strong.
Their claws are sharp.

Habitat

Komodo dragons live in Indonesia. It is hot and dry there. They swim between small islands.

Where Komodo dragons live

Food

Komodo dragons eat small animals.

Their tongues "taste" the air.
This helps them find prey.

They hide and wait for prey.
Then they jump out.
They bite and claw the prey.

Life Cycle

Female Komodo dragons
lay eggs in holes.

They guard the eggs.
Babies **hatch** from the eggs.

Babies live on their own.
They climb trees.

This keeps them safe. They can live for 30 years in the wild.

Average Weight

A Komodo dragon weighs almost as much as a refrigerator.

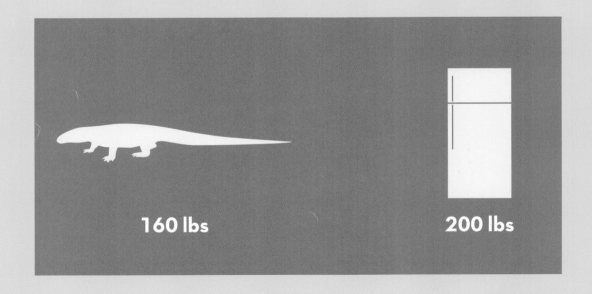

160 lbs   200 lbs

Average Length

A male Komodo dragon is longer than a sofa.

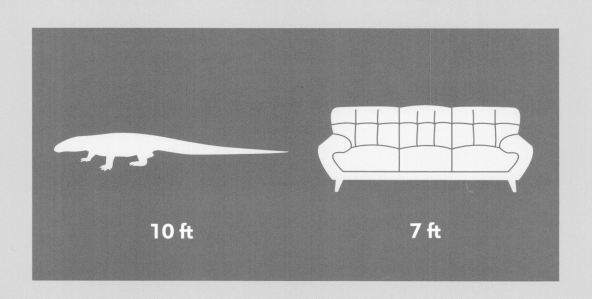

10 ft   7 ft

Glossary

bacteria – tiny living things that break down plant or animal matter.

cold-blooded – getting its body temperature from the outside.

hatch – to be born from an egg.

prey – an animal that is hunted and eaten by another animal.

reptile – a cold-blooded animal with scales. They typically lay eggs.

Booklinks

For more information on
Komodo dragons, please visit
booklinks.abdopublishing.com

Z⊕m In on Animals!

Learn even more with the Abdo Zoom
Animals database. Check out
abdozoom.com for more information.

Index